WE **STILL** LEAVE A LEGACY

Philip Robinson

Copyright © 2017 by Philip Robinson

All rights reserved
This book or any portion shall thereof
may not be reproduced or used in any manner whatsoever
without the express written permission of the author
except for the use of brief quotations in a book review.

Printed in the United States of America

ISBN-978-0-692-78293-4

Contact

We Still Leave a Legacy Press
Phrobin417@aol.com

Poet's Photo

Craig Bailey: Perspective Photo
PerspectivePhoto. net

Book Design

TreeHouse Studio

About the Author

Philip started writing poetry in the late 1960's during his years as an undergraduate at Emerson College. He continued this new-found personal self-expression through graduate school at Boston College. Presently, Philip looks upon his writing as a therapeutic tool to assist him through life passages. He is also happy to share his work with others. He has had his first book of poems, *Secret Passages A Trilogy of Thought* published in the late 1980's. He is anthologized in *The Road Before US: 100 Gay Black Poets, In The Life: A Black Gay Anthology, When the Drama Club Is Not Enough, The Last Closet the real lives of lesbian and gay teachers,* and *Life in Our Own Words*. Philip completed his next book of poems, *In The Trenches: The Voice of a Guidance Counselor* due out in 2017. This next book will chronicle in part Philip's long 32 years as an educator/guidance counselor for Boston Public Schools. He and his partner of 35 years, Joseph Jackson, are both retired from Boston Public Schools. They live in West Roxbury, MA.

Foreword

When I started to write *We Still Leave a Legacy*, it was with a heavy heart. I had these friends of mine, some of them fellow writers like myself, taken away by this pandemic known as HIV/AIDS. It was like an emotional roller-coaster ride. The deaths happened frequently and with great stress. I couldn't imagine at times the enormity of pain that consumed so many of us as we were left to grieve. I also knew other friends and family members who had died from varied sicknesses. So in midst of this storm, I felt the way to remember the masses of people, was through their personal contributions left to us. I vowed to reflect and never lose sight of those individuals that entered my life.
Hence, that is how I came up with the title.

I also found my voice by opening myself up to the lasting gifts given to me. It is still becoming a stronger and more vocal one. It's a voice that speaks about the past, the present and the future with a sense of faith and hope. We must never give up the fight for those personal dreams, to strive to develop projects that benefits others, and of course simply, and equally important continue to love oneself.

I know by the grace of God that there are people whose shoulders I stand on and walk with in a daily way. It is in this sense of clarity of guidance, I will never walk alone.

Acknowledgments

Philip Robinson's *We Still Leave a Legacy* offers us a glimpse into a time that is not yet passed. It also captures the pain that lingers as we reflect on the lives of those who were unable to fulfill their potential as a result of unforeseen and unnatural interference. It is a powerful labor of effort as Philip fights through that pain to bring us a vision of the very special people in his life whom he loves and has lost.

We often think of "Legacy" as that which is left behind. As I reflect on We Still Leave a Legacy, I am struck by the notion of how rarely we give attention to the evolution of a legacy. What are the incredible qualities an individual engenders that causes them to be a legacy in the making? Philip has been my friend for almost forty years. In this period of time, I feel that I have been privileged to know a very steadfastly creative individual. Philip has made a wonderfully honorable tribute to those whose lives have been significant to him. He has also unselfishly devoted his life to important causes with sincere compassion, love, and gentle devotion. Philip does this while embracing all of us with tender encouragement to be better invested in our own creativity. Philip is one of the very few people in my life who pushes me beyond the precipice of my apparent self to be all that I can be and more.

George H. Campbell
New York, New York

A must read book. This gifted poet and educator continues to be a compelling voice not only for those seeking true self-identity and equality; but also for those who died while on this arduous quest.

—Pat Council
Portland, Maine

Phil lets us into his inner sanctum with unbridled emotion, passion and a voice that made me laugh, cry and even cheer for the boldness of his words. His poems are rooted in a reality we all need to understand and embrace.

—Carrie H. Johnson
Hot Flash, a novel
From the Pits to the Palace

We Still Leave a Legacy is a volume inspired in part by the HIV/AIDS epidemic, and the people Philip has worked with, loved and lost. It gives us a very personal perspective on this devastating disease and the lives it still effects, including his own. Philip's writings, also reminds us of the various forms of life's experiences. One particular poem that leapt off the page for me was "Confession". Philip writes about his mother's dementia. I am intimately familiar with how this disease affects not only the victim, but the family as well. It evokes a profound memory for me, and is indicative of the gift Philip possesses to touch us with his words. I am honored to be a part of his journey!

—Ahmasi R. Lloyd
New York, New York

Dedication

I sincerely dedicate this book
to my dear friend and partner of 36 years,
Joseph Jackson. He continues to guide me through
these passages of life with kindness, patience and love.

WE **STILL** LEAVE A LEGACY

Contents

Awakened	17
Simpatico	18
The Battle	19
Camille	21
He Lives Within Us	22
The Other Side of Dying	23
By Definition	24
Is There a Bullet with My Name?	25
Unlit Candles	27
Grover Cleveland Middle School-Memories	29
Confession	31
In Midst of a Storm	32
Etiquette	33
Beyond Therapy	35
The Gift	36
The Legacy She Creates	37
Brothers du Jour	39
Standing Amongst My Heroes	40
Vicarious Thrust	41
Connected Road	42
Attached	43
Inheritance	44
The Call	46

In The Public and Private Domains	48
The Streets Roar	50
Diane's Light	51
Growing From the Milestone	53
Posthumous	55
No Mystery to Love	56
The Escape	57
Shanelle's Song	58
Walk the Talk	59
Immediate Family	60
Template	61
Balancing the Imbalance	62
No Apologies	65
Wise Tale	67
Beginnings	68
The Scar	69
Furor	70
Investment	72
Curtain Call	73
Consequences	75
Dodging Bullets	76
Invest	77
If We Were Girlfriends	78
Solidarity	80
Malignancy	81

Memory in Motion	82
Pantheon	83
When I Stopped Kissing My Father	85
Perform	86
Who Saves Us?	88
Great Minds	90
Surrender	91
The Weight	92
The Habit	94
The Past Returns	95
Power	96
Resonance	97
The Love Affair	98
Tribute	99
The Final Bell	101
We Still Leave a Legacy	102
No God-No Boundaries	103
The Aftermath	105
The Visit	106
Paradoxical	107
The Spirit of Remembrance	108
Landscape	109

Awakened

I woke up with the urge to write and found blood on the floor.
The cold bottoms of my feet met the moisture and my heart skipped a beat.
The trail's drippings were warm and wet.
The drench sensation merged with the carpet's beige Shetland.
I ran the course which led me to the opened door.
I saw my cousin Terence pasted against the field
wielding a knife in his right hand.
"Don't save me!" He yelled. "I'm sick of this fucking curse AIDS.
It's going to kill us all!"
Frightened by the shadows, I rushed back to bed.
I pretended and hoped this was a
nightmare.

Simpatico

You were feeding my soul,
until death took you away.
Sadness permeated my every pore.
Then I remembered our conversations,
when we talked about everything—
our darkest days, the brief fulfilling moments,
the silly crushes, and those fleeting dreams.
I see those days even clearer now.
We rode to the hospital holding
hands and singing along with Chaka:
—*Through the fire to the limit...*
I cried nonstop. You asked me why there were so many tears.
Yet, you knew.
This was that magic God created.
I remembered our all-night chatter and your ceaseless snoring.
We shared the congested air.
Your Meal on Wheels was our last supper.
You retreated when I said I had to leave.
I promised to return,
and I did.
I just didn't know it would be our final goodbye.
You have a permanent home in my heart.

The Battle

"My eyes have seen the glory of the coming of the Lord."

Change, we hear, is the pulse of the movement.
But we have today's black ministers preaching separation.
They advocate a constitutional freeze on social change.
Paradoxes come to mind when they dare say,
Be happy, but don't destroy the black family structure with this
same-sex-wanting-to-get-married stuff.
My father's womanizing and drunkenness broke up my parent's marriage
His lifestyle almost killed my mother.
These ministers profess to be radical and idealistic in their thinking.
Yet, many of them questioned the existence of AIDS when it arrived at their
churches' doorsteps.
One can't preach truth and hatred in the same voice.
What minister has stepped into Rev. Martin King's shoes?
Rev. King's unparalleled wisdom, his tremendous courage, and deep commitment
to civil rights hasn't been inherited.
We sing.
We also commit ourselves to God and pledge ties to our churches, only
to hear that we are thieves.
Taking what? From whom?
How can the church stand on solid ground
while teaching bigotry and intolerance?
While throwing rocks at those it professes to love?
Loving someone of the same gender does not render each of us
One-fifth of a human being.
We want to carry that love into marriage,
for love's sake and to guarantee our basic civil rights.
It's downright unjust to discriminate against us on this basis!
We continue to let our monies be used
for wars that haven't freed us,
We continue to pay
for guns and drugs that kill our youth,
thereby robbing those black families of their hopes and dreams.

We learned that each generation
is more accepting and tolerant of differences.

The truth should be marching on.

I believe God rode into town to save my soul
as well as others.
He intended for humanity to be united in love,
not divided by hate. Since God made all of us in His image,
we are all part of humanity.
So this American President will have to explain
how rights accorded to straight folks
can be denied to gay couples.
Please explain why I have no right to visit my partner in the hospital,
when he is in ICU,
Explain why I have no right to sponsor a loved one for immigration,
Explain why I have no right to my partner's social security, family and medical
benefits, the automatic inheritance,
Explain why you will only grant me marriage in modified forms,
but never in name,
Explain how my having sex with a male
nullifies my right to become a blood donor to others?
The criteria for healing the sick,
shouldn't have anything to do with my sexual fulfillment.
Please explain to me the kind of thinking that underlies these policies.
When did love become a battle
that must be constantly fought?

Camille

"I am beautiful, no matter what they say, words won't bring me down."

But they did for Camille; so much that she stayed home from school and got sick.
So began her
spiral descent
into failure.
Camille wrestled with the question of whether she would be better off dead.
The taunts from other students, their lies, and even threats
were all eating away at her soul.
She felt her sense of hope being destroyed.
Yet, by American standards of beauty, Camille
is a knock-out!
Other girls envied her chiseled cheekbones and long-flowing hair.
She also has that old Coke-A-Cola bottle body.
The Commodores song—*Brickhouse*—comes to mind.
Camille couldn't see her own beauty, and didn't believe in herself.
It was as if her mirror needed to be fixed so Camille could see the
strength of her inner spirit.
But to Camille's credit, she went to the mentor program to begin
the healing process.
No point in her singing this song if she doesn't believe in herself.

He Lives Within Us All

James Baldwin spoke from Giovanni's Room, a bittersweet upsurge to the
discovery of self.
It will never be a forgotten purpose.
Baldwin's piercing voice spoke to us about us.
It talked about our right to excel to and to thrive
on that rhythm.
He gave the souls of black folk to white people for them
to examine their own true beings.
Baldwin embellished the meaning of "truth" since he had to develop it
constantly with those who didn't understand Black worth.
He breathed life into lifeless forms, forcing them to see and become
part of something real—something that could easily pass you by
if you remained still.
"Challenge not to be mediocre," Baldwin said.
Author and activist, Imamu Amiri Baraka said, "Jimmy is God's revolutionary
mouth if there is a God."
Baraka also said that Jimmy traveled the earth like a historian---observing,
analyzing, documenting. Jimmy used his beautiful way with words to beam a
powerful spotlight on the most neglected social and political issues of the day.
In doing so he challenged us to think outside the box and to be better than what
we are. Jimmy made us consciously human; or perhaps more acidly pre-human.
Baldwin's collection of works is one of my twentieth century treasures that
no one can ever destroy.
There is an eternal baptism to his words. Praises are due to the preacher
that never died within him.
Baldwin's death still presents us with America's contradiction.
His rage is my rage.
Our mission is to continue witnessing and writing about institutionalized
and individual tyranny.
He is the good news we need to spread.
So, go tell it on the mountain,
and never forget him.
He means too much.

The Other Side of Dying!

Each man's death is a sober reminder we all have a number.
Some get called right away. Others pursue, conquer, and share their blessings.
Then they don't have to cry when saying goodbye; because
they have planted something others will watch over as it grows.
However, there are those who sit as the clock ticks away.
They ponder and otherwise contribute nothing to the very earth they live on.
When my father died years ago, people cursed and scream…some prayed.
In those silent requests to "Dear God," it was asked that no one else go like
my Dad.
He was poor, sick and not remembered honorably!
It was heart sickening to say the least.
Dad's oldest sister, our distant aunt, was there meeting nieces and nephews
for the first time. She shouted out,
"Hey, he was already dead in my eyes!"
Suffering a loss is one thing;
another is fighting hard amongst each other because we're unable to cover
expenses.
Two other aunts pointed fingers, blaming everyone else
for their brother's demise.
Fighting hard!
There was no church funeral, not even a hired minister
to promise a life hereafter.
I wrote a poem in his honor and read it to make peace;
but no one else allowed their tears to flow.
The pain was too intense for anyone to offer up forgiveness.
No one stopped their daily routines.
After all, this was a different day.
This death caused people to battle with their own sense of mortality.
The imprint of one's life is etched in hearts that are left behind
to remember.

By Definition

If I miss a day of laughter, I know
sadness will sweep into my life.
I notice people's faces light up when a smile introduces me to them.
Sealing ourselves off by not appreciating laughter
means we just take things too seriously.
My friend Kathy's laughter,
along with mine,
resonates throughout the house.
People either stand and admire our connection,
wish to join us, or they dismiss it as an intrusion to the stillness.
We should link up with those who can make us laugh.
It's a chance to part the sea between good and bad.
It's no surprise that the people we meet with such attributes,
add to our lives and contribute to the sum total of who we become.
We can never say that laughter kills anyone.

Is There A bullet with my Name?

"One man's death diminishes you." John Donne

On any given day gunshots
erupt below my window
and outside my door as
I enter into my sanctuary.
"Six people shot, one dead and the other five barely holding on,
after back-to-back nights of inner city violence," the reporter states.

Details are sketchy. No suspects have been found.
There were only bodies riddled with bullets
in the neck, waist, groin, and hip. How did they miss the heart?
Those bodies were once filled with love,
or perhaps hate.
Maybe those who shot have no one of their own.
The mayor claims shooting and homicides are down.

How do you reconcile that with the deceased?
These victims can't say.
Their voices have been taken away.

Spilled blood on the street marks
the territory where illegal drugs and illegal
weapons co-exist like the mice
that feed off garbage.
The proliferation of this traffic intensifies.
No one tells us how to stop the sale of guns.
Saying no to drugs is still not happening.
"What gun shops do you know of in the black communities?"
questioned the wise old man sitting on the bench.
Fear was preventing him from his daily walks.

"It's like we are in our own little Iraq.
Do I need to fight an unknown enemy

or the one that robs
and threatens my immediate security.
Has urban warfare waved a curse over us all?
Who pulled the triggers
on those once happy innocent souls?
Where is the next bullet headed?
Is watching my back enough
of a guard?"

Unlit Candles

Wrapped and tucked away are numerous gifts with bows tied.
Scattered around is colorful landscape-like wrapping paper,
small boxes, for the demure fragile things, and big boxes
for the must-be-at-home delivery types.

I remember vividly the bash your family planned and threw
for your arrival
back home.
Throngs of people came. Some were curious to see you
up front and alive!
The cars parked on the family grass didn't cause any
disturbance;
there was so much happiness just being in your midst.

There are no streets bearing your name.
Posthumously, no awards are given to those who aspire
to be just like you—
writer, activist, and humanitarian.
You always said if we were kind to life, peace would follow.
You wrote and talked about that passionately.
Boy, did you save some souls!

I hold onto the date of your birth as if I delivered you!
How could anyone forget?
To honor your birth is to sing praises
of the love you gave us.
Twelve years later, your day is still important.

Days leading up to your special natal one, are ironically filled
with the birth dates of other fallen warriors and friends.
Steven Corbin wrote about "Fragments That Remain."
It's a story about his many loves that got away.
He vowed to never let me out of his sight.
That was his last expressed sentiment.

I am comforted to know Steven's spirit visits me.
Assotto Saint's poetic Haitian cry outed those voices
that were silenced by their death.
He asserted "AIDS can't take away their dignity.
Their lives meant too much."

Assotto further preached about what ministers omitted from
too many eulogies: "One's sexuality shouldn't be
on trial as they are being laid to rest."
His words, like fire, extinguished borders long associated with HIV/AIDS.

James Baldwin said, "The moment we break faith with one another,
the sea engulfs us and the light goes out."

My own brother's birthday is but a mere whisper,
if mentioned at all.
Dennis's death shattered my mother's heart.
Her sister says it will never heal.
My mother can't even call out Dennis's name without falling over
and crying profusely.

I shall always celebrate Dennis's birthday.
Death can't take that too;
because with it came a lasting friendship that still lights up in my heart.

Grover Cleveland Middle School—Memories

If these walls could talk, they would speak of the lessons still being taught;
of curriculums and paradigms developed to move
the goal of freedom forward through education.
They would also talk about the solid services delivered by competent teachers and counselors who are legendary. These professionals have always been eager to share their wealth to the next generation.
If these walls could talk, they would document students' achievements and willingness to learn despite challenges faced while growing up. They would also document students' constructive efforts to conquer fear and their desire to travel at their own pace.
We always wanted to hear their young and impressionable voices;
so we encouraged them to speak out.
These walls hold such memories.

If these walls could talk, they would give testament to the most motivated, intelligent cadre of principals: Barry, Carty, Lyons, Abbott, Downey, Sidberry, Duarte, Hanscom, Jones, and our present day warrior Andy Tuite,
who is ever so compassionate.
This building has been held up through their exemplary
we-are-here-to-serve forces.
If these walls could talk, they would say we had fought the good fight
in addressing, when possible, numerous "presenting issues."
After each issue was tackled, the students knew we had their backs.
The support was infinite.
We wrestled with new ideas. Some we won. Others failed.
We never feared embarking upon a newer course of action.

Each person contributed to the passing of the torch.
The fire within us all burned for the love of the school
and for the love of the kids;
even when the students couldn't believe they could love themselves.

And so we stand at the end of this day,
never really saying goodbye to experiences that made us each stronger.

We stand committed to this form of social change. Education remains the answer to fulfilling dreams.
We have come from Scituate, Weymouth, Hingham, Canton, Milton, Hyde Park, West Roxbury, Brockton, Randolph, Quincy, Roslindale, East Boston, South Boston, Dorchester, Mattapan, and Roxbury.
The Grover Cleveland Middle School's doors welcomed us all.
Our arms – those of us teachers, administrators, support staff—remained opened.

They embraced the thousands of young minds that came and graduated.
Those youth went on to passionately remember, as we all do, that
Grover Cleveland Middle School shines;
because we never let it do anything else!

Confession

I call my mother less these days.
It has become a contradiction of sorts for me.
I tell my students at school,
"Do not take these times for granted, tomorrow is never promised.
Tell those you love you can't live without them, even when you know someday you'll have to try."
But could I walk the talk and not feel it?
The calls are not as frequent; because mom has a difficult time processing everything.
When we attempt to talk, I can feel her pressure rising
through her voice.
She conjures up those old stories that should have died years ago.
Alas the past, or is it life, lives on through the vision of memory.
I can attest to a person's good intentions. Yet all my mother
sees is the dark side of that same person.
It is clear to us, her five kids, that she is not listening anymore
when we talk; or are we believing her sense of timing is off
and assuming our paths will follow in this order?
Aging and genes can't be too incorrect.
My mom and I used to cry, laugh together and even look forward
to the next call.
My sister reminds me, "Mom was there when we needed her!"
I know my mother is destined to part this earth, as will I.
Yet these are not the times to take her for granted.
Her purpose as our mother has not been fulfilled, I tell myself.
I dial her number hoping to hear her voice.

In the Midst Of a Storm

It's a feeling I have whenever the weather
decides to rain on my parade. You will cover me, and I'll walk a thousand more miles.
It's a feeling that surrounds me
when my doubts about other friendships shake my soul. I see
the confidence in your eyes and in your effervescent smile.
I know your embrace strengthens my spirit. Hey, I am renewed.
I know it goes beyond this moment and that you have no qualms about
telling me your love will never cease.
So I say, bring on the storm.

Etiquette

Whenever Derrick visited the Sinclair household,
Roscoe's parents retired to their bedroom and shut the door. The Sinclairs are a working-class family.
They have been married for 33 years and lived in the housing projects, where Mr. Sinclair has been a janitor for 25 years.
Mrs. Sinclair works as a secretary in a downtown Manhattan law firm. The Sinclairs had a daughter Jasmine and a son Roscoe.
Jasmine died in an auto accident 15 years ago.
Roscoe was in his senior year at New York University majoring in English Literature and Journalism.
Roscoe was excited about his acceptance to Boston University's graduate school
next year.
Whenever his friend Derrick came over to the Sinclair house, Roscoe was filled with trepidation.
Derrick is adamant that the two must sleep together and make love.
Roscoe's fear puzzled Derrick.
He felt if Roscoe's parents can make love; then hell, why can't they?
However, Derrick hollered out, "Shit, yeah, shit, yeah!"
in the heat of their passion-filled moments.
So he promised his lover he would bite the tip of the pillowcase whenever the stuff got so hot and good to him.
Roscoe wasn't too certain that would work. What if the pillowcase slipped? What if his father, who is in poor health, heard him and had a heart attack?
The thought scattered Roscoe.
On the other hand, Derrick lived with his widowed, southern-born, strictly-from the-bible mother; four younger siblings; three sisters; and an overachieving, noisy brother.
His household was already cramped.
One warm August evening, Derrick visited Roscoe. He asked, "Am I spending the night?"
Roscoe, a bit hesitant at first, said, "Yes. But no sex! Okay?"
Derrick wanted to go off.
But he counted to a silent ten and said "Okay, no sex!"

When Roscoe's parents went into their bedroom and closed the door that night,
Roscoe and Derrick also retired. Faster than Pedro Martinez' pitch, Derrick got all over Roscoe, who offered little resistance.
The sex lasted hours. Roscoe got so caught up in the rapture and in Derrick's "Shit, yeah, shit, yeah!" that he climaxed.
Now Mrs. Sinclair, Roscoe and Derrick
are sitting soberly in the hospital emergency room.
The strength of her Jamaican upbringing and self-control is holding them all together.
The doctor comes in and tells them Mr. Sinclair will be all right, He only suffered a mild stroke.

Clearly, the next time Derrick and Roscoe spend the night together it will be in their own apartment.
No one's health should be compromised or sleep interrupted.

Beyond Therapy

Annie Lee and her brother Jian are sick and tired of their perpetually Black Asian hair.
Saleeda's discontentment about her African-American roots runs deep. She hates the way her hair grows or doesn't grow.
If you are like these individuals, then maybe
adding not only a little bit of color but those brunette extensions might make you fit right in.
In fact, a simple dye-job, which highlights and accentuates the presumed positive, can allow you to cross over.
No one said you have to put up with anything longer than usual nowadays.
In fact, you can literally take away whole body parts that don't "represent" you. It is now possible to
suck out thighs, flatten stomachs,
tuck chins, clip ears, and put back eyes.
You will definitely cause other people to raise their eyes in disbelief. You can hide from the aging process, replace it with
something else, and still call yourself the same person. This is done all in the name of vanity,
or non-acceptance,
or showing defiance with a twist of resentment. Hey! It beats lying on a couch.
You do not have to tell a therapist how you hate your body, dislike your parents for their gene pool, and despise the doctor who delivered you!

The Gift

"I would be nothing if I couldn't sing my song."

When Johnny Mathis sings,
it's like no one else
I have ever heard.
He sings so sweetly; even the birds listen.
"Chances are…"
I would give anything to hear
Ella scat again
Or even sing her winning song,
" A tisket, a tasket.
I sold my yellow basket."
That voice of Donny Hathaway! Wow! I can hear him proclaim, "Talking about the ghetto…" which is still alive and well.
Drugs fester and dreams die there every day.
Did Donny jump from that building; so he could see the other side and return?
I wish I could hear Judy Garland's rendition of "Somewhere Over The Rainbow."
Was it too far for her to believe it was there?
I have nightly concerts of Lady Day serenading me.
"Them that got shall get." "Them that not shall lose."
"So the bible says, and it's still news."
Minnie Riperton sang "Loving you is sweeter than a dream come true."
Who could contest such a feeling?
Marvin Gaye spoke of the injustices in "What's Going On?" and compelled us to question life.
His own father, or was it God, shortened Marvin's time on this earth. Phyllis Hyman's "Somewhere in my Lifetime" and "You Know How to Love Me" didn't save her soul.
I wish I could hear those voices again!

The Legacy She Creates

With her "I see trees of green….red roses too!
I see them bloom…for me and for you, and I say to myself
What a wonderful world."

Our spaces would not be complete without her presence.
She dances into our lives with familiar and enduring names, MeeMee,
mommy, aunt, and great aunt too, cousin,
and of course dear friend.
She has these many titles (length of time on earth notwithstanding); because
she has earned each one!
We grow with her endless loves that foster all things good and righteous. She
lives to give us lessons on how to treat others with kindness.
She challenges us to live life fully; no drama, no mystery. Then our souls
become complete.
She spins hope into the brew we drink.
She talks with clarity making sense of things we couldn't possibly know.
"Don't ponder, you'll miss the beat."
She advocates for the sick, neglecting herself.
But God's just reward for her is a renewed heart that ticks away to
the beat of seasons.
Step with her sense of optimism which inspires us to become that person
she has been for her 90 years.
Numerous souls are being nurtured with her sense of self-assuredness. The
strength of her being adds to our foundations.
In trying to keep up with her, no one would dispute her knowledge or history
of the family.
In fact, sit with her and she'll give it to you straight up and uncensored.
Her mind is active, because she rolls with the young, the old and all those
in-between.
Do not ever attempt to fool her with gifts of something she already possesses.
"I have five or six of those things down in the basement."
Humor, laughter and candor are her forte'

So we rally around her today to express our continued love, and to honor her. Never forsake this wonderful treasure.

You are the best of what anyone of us could ever be. Thank you for the gift of you.

"The skies are blue…clouds of white

brighted blessed days…dark sacred nights."

And I say to myself you have made us such a wonderful world!

Brothers du Jour: (from left to right: Thomas Grimes, Roy Gonsalves and Philip Robinson)

Standing Amongst My Heroes

I remember Thomas' funeral, the church packed to the rim.
People came literally from all walks of life, congregated in sadness and remembrance.
Thomas had met numerous souls along the way.
Who hadn't heard his exciting actor's voice once or twice! Thomas was determined to read in front of Kings and Queens. He and I laughed, prayed and wanted desperately to take
our show of performance poetry on the road.
Oprah, we felt, really hadn't heard words like ours.
I think back to Thomas' final day he laid there in royal state. Naomi, appeared late, her usual, to perform in this sacred setting. Maurice and Joan were there. They represented the Writers of Color. Clearly, they are the other pillars in my life.
My good friend Jean sat again at another funeral; a friend of her late son Roy. Thomas, Roy and I read together, and Jean had the last picture
of us at the event on her refrigerator.
Her daughter Yvonne said that photo had bad karma and it should be taken down, since I was the only one left.
I waited my turn to read.
It was difficult to say good-bye through verse to a dear soul-mate friend.
I sang to ready my voice for the emotional impact of my words.
As I finished, I felt a need to warn folks, "Don't short-change Thomas with your silly expressions of grief."
He deserved much more.
Whenever Thomas spoke, it was pure gospel. His words ringed with joy. Folks felt anointed by the truth. He lifted me up so many times.
I have one less voice through his demise.
Yet, I know I stand on his shoulders and beside others. My heroes never leave me.

Vicarious Thrust

Dwayne speeded towards me as if he were on roller skates--- dodging the light, blinding my path faster than flash.
I thought his escalating energy was related to
the school's
headmaster leaving for good, or about an abrupt dismissal enabling him to pick up the latest Usher's jam. Whatever it was, he felt compelled to share this hot-off-the-press report.
He was the self-appointed envoy.
His new dreadlocks were like little nubs on a wilted plant. His larger-than-life green and purple Gap shirt flowed over his 4 ft. 11 in. frame.
All of his thirty-twos sparkled a wholesome unblemished quality.
"Mr. Robinson," he halted, while attempting to speak and breathe together.
"Latisha said you have a big butt."
I kept walking.
"Dudded big butt" has become my new title.
"Here she is!" his voice echoed with excitement down the long corridor.
Dwayne pumped out his chest as if his goal had been accomplished
To this day, I haven't seen or heard word one from Latisha.

Connected Road

Jake said I spoke too much about the "spirits" being Gods that watched over us even in the midst of our personal battles.
Solomon proclaimed I didn't know diddly squat about playing bid whist. In fact, he said that Ingrid beat the shit out of me when we were in college.
"Hell, she beat everyone!" I responded.
Jerome couldn't stand for me to write about our love nest.
He felt sharing with others violated our space. So he would state with strong compassion:
"Never hang your laundry out because others will take it and run with it. They'll even claim you never had it, if it's too good!"
David was coming to visit me one moonlit evening.
I had 30 candles burning to symbolize the days we had been together. I also had his favorite wine chilling.
The serenading music kept my love aglow. David had a car accident racing to see me. How could I not love him back?
Now, I had to speed out to see him.
I held his hands and kissed him gently as he laid in his hospital bed.
His parents sat beside him too.
They were in pain but managed to smile. Their support was insurmountable.
They also witnessed our love, and felt David made a good choice. I did too.

Attachment

There were times, Karen and I served as Belynda's
health care proxies.
We met her deadlines and assisted her in deciding to postpone the pain.
Sadly, during Belynda's eleventh hour in another town, we were reduced to
mere "no" voices back in Boston. We were prepared to cross city lines.
However, her family's trust finally fell.

Steven, the gifted writer, felt he would see me again.
He said he would write about our adventures. Steven also planned to
personally show me Paris,
his favorite city.
His death silenced his thoughts. God had other plans.
Our lovemaking had to wait too.

Roy's family became my own. His loving mother and siblings established
such a bond with me.
My union with them keeps Roy's spirit alive.
Our niece, Royelle, gave me tissues to dry my eyes.

Thomas's pride prevented him from turning to me. He didn't want help any
more.
He must have known I would have given my heart to save him.
His sister knew our love was like no other.
My tears are felt whenever his name is spoken.

Bill's music! I called it that because it was
he who introduced me to those mezzo-sopranos, the pillars and divas of song.
I never would have heard them on my own. Today, whenever I hear those
majestic voices,
I know it's Bill telling me to keep on listening.

Inheritance

It was strange in many ways.
Some of these relatives have never traveled miles upon miles on airplanes before.
Then there were other family members
who lived in the same town and had not spoken to one another in many years.
Yet here they were—all 19 of them—assembled and ready to bear witness.
Sara, the matriarch of the Bartlett family, had died peacefully.
She was an 87-year-old, singularly optimistic, free-spirited woman.

It was time to read her will.
Sara Bartlett had inherited a large
amount of money from her late husband Theodore.
For 48 years the Bartlett's had owned the largest
black funeral home this side of the New England Turnpike.

When the time came, no one was ready to take over the business. Nathaniel Bartlett, the youngest son of Teddy and Sara, had attempted in his feeble way to operate the "home," as they called it.
But Nat sometimes appeared to be too caught up with his own pursuit of stage acting.
His Aunt Anita always called his fleeting pipe dream,
"pretending-to-work."
Nat's brother and sister, Michelle and Teddy Jr., felt the funeral
home gave them chills. "Your father spent many long years struggling to keep the three of you off the welfare lines. How could you let that struggle go up in smoke?" Aunt Anita would often ponder this out loud, wherever and whenever
the spirit hit her.

The lawyer entered the room and greeted the family members. Some were in their Sunday finest.
"Hello Bartlett family. I would like to start the reading of Mrs. Sara
Lois Bartlett's will."
The shuffling of chairs and clearing of throats ensued. Harris Benson was the

family lawyer for too many years.
In fact, folks often thought he and Teddy Sr. were brothers.

"Well. I, Sara Lois Bartlett, in my most solid of mind, leave behind my worldly belongings—like clothes and household items--- to the Goodwill and the
Big Brother and Big Sister organizations . . ."
Sighs resonated.
"I also leave the following possessions to the Nigerian Health Fund to distribute
as they see fit: the money from my estate which is in excess of $2 million, the Bartlett Funeral Home, and my house which some of you have called too pristine."

The Call
(Nurturing the Spirit)

"I'll be somewhere listening for my name."

My world appears to be closing in on me. There is a voice lost each day to AIDS.
Reading the daily obit pages leaves me shattered. I cry, run and come back to my own suffering.

Friends out of my inner circle ponder silently about my own health status.
I hide nothing.
I want to say, "No, things are not all right. The chiseling away at my life has left
me numb. Goddammit I'm in pain."
There is no invisible way of conveying my anger and my rage. Is there a need to go on?

I read Assotto Saint's plea for help, page after page.
He hollered out for recognition, even from his coffin.
"Save my fellow Haitians. Give my remaining friends a cure. Don't let blood continue to flow!"
Roy Gonsalves screamed, "The hell with AIDS Education!"
The repeated memorial services presented me with memorable written verse.
I have cried a thousand tears on sleeves and borrowed tissues.
I cannot say my soul is cleansed.

These deaths are like gaping holes that sink deep. I count the endless lives taken from me.
Yes, it is personal.
The stage we read upon has become emptier.
I miss their specific voices and their performances.

Harold Robinson, a cousin through the word, said, "In the midst of a storm, as our grief consumes us, we must remember to nurture the spirits. If we close down, we'll never be able to leave anything behind."
He further said we have to rise up, fight back
and fear no one despite our losses.
We have come this far.
I'll just keep calling out their names.

In the Public and Private Domains

Twenty-five years this June, the calendar will proclaim that we have come this far and we still have not found an answer. Twenty-five years! As Violet would say metaphorically,
"Yes. We have turned some corners only to confront that same element while traveling in those corners."
Twenty-five years later, and some folks can't believe AIDS is not a man-made device meant to destroy the world. How big a bomb do we need? There are those who also contend that maybe it's the pharmaceutical big boys' ploy to control us through medication.
In clear view, many thousands have gone. Under Reagan's careful watch and avoidance money needed for research, went elsewhere.
In the past 25 years we have seen this pandemic blanket the map. Not one country is being spared.
Silence and fear permeate the country. The judging game rests in some minds.
Who will be revealed when their past returns?
Phill Wilson is a survivor, activist, and a free speech advocate. He says, "Stand up and proudly state you are HIV-positive." Look how AA's mantra revealed that "disease" to society.
Phill believes a public stance on a private illness unifies us. Twenty-five years later and the black churches are just beginning to open their doors stating, "We are all God's children. Please
accept our apologies for closing our places of worship to you so fast." In 25 years my world has never experienced such an enormous personal loss. Friends died each month.
Talk about endless memorial services!
One catholic priest protested, "There can't be too many speakers."
Hey, we continued to read our poems of remembrance and sing our songs. We just about took over the churches. Maybe that was their fear.
However, it was at those crucial times that we were attempting to "heal thyself"

and come to grips with this unstoppable plague.
Will I be able to tell the next generation I did something to help find a cure?
Can we collectively stand and publicly say,
"HIV/AIDS affects us all!"
Maybe lives will be saved.

The Streets Roar

I assumed you knew the revolution is being televised!
Even as you shut off the tube, it still came out on all levels.
Fourteen-year-old JR is stabbed three times, minutes after school closed on a bright Tuesday afternoon.
Fast Forward to Friday and 17-year-old Amanda was slashed by a jilted suitor during her early morning arrival to school.
Then the assailant stabbed himself and collapsed. He wanted her love back. Did he think her death would return it?
Two separate high school proms were cancelled; the so-called tradition of segregating the races had to cease. One hundred-fifty students suffered the loss. A
13-year-old Groveland youth was accused of molesting two young seven and eight-year-old girls.
Madrid's terrorist killed 191 and injured 1,890.
Four American civilians were shot dead and dragged down a Baghdad street.
Oklahoma's bombing destroyed and crumbled lives young and old. The Columbine High School massacre buried dreams and made schools questionable safe havens.
A coal mine explosion in Beijing killed 35 people.
Thailand defended Islamic militants suspected of murdering 108 people.
Speculation unfolded that an Islamic separatist movement began to re-emerge.
Macedonian police gunned down seven innocent immigrants.
They contend these individuals were terrorists.
In Ankara, Turkey, a young 14-year-old girl is strangled by her own father.
He contends he wanted to restore family honor. This was after his daughter had been kidnapped and raped.
One wound healed; another inflicted. One wound healed; another inflicted…

Diane's Light

"This little light of mine, I'm going to let it shin. This little light of mine, I'm going to let it shine."

—My life's light hasn't always been dim.
Those haunting and sometimes harsh voices I have heard, laid dormant. I never knew I would need two pills a day
to quiet them.
But, my life's light hasn't always been dim. I was able to shine it when
I taught for more than 20 years. This anchored me and made me feel whole.
I bestowed upon my bilingual students and others
a sense of wisdom and knowledge. Hopefully that allowed them to grow into productive
and contributing citizens of the world.
Every teacher wants to believe that they are in these young minds' lives to make a difference. I left the school each day feeling like I had
done a service to humanity.
I applauded these students. They gave me an opportunity to grow with them. We learned from one another.
I want to thank the next set of people from the bottom of my heart and soul with all the fiber in me. They are my cousins, the Morris family—Michelle, Glenn, Miles, and Dale-
—and their extended family members. Extra special thanks goes out to my indomitable
Aunt Elaine for being there with me from the very beginning to the end.
They were there when I argued and cursed
them out ferociously.
They saw and begged me to stop the smoking and excessive shopping. Did I really need two of everything?
However, my heart did allow me to extend myself. As I gave gifts to others, I felt their joy!
Please understand. These diversions fed me in ways that only a person with no sense of boundaries could
know about.

Aunt Elaine, you were there. You wanted me to realize and accept my total being
without losing sight of the bridges I have crossed. You took me to the numerous medical appointments. Doctors would
marvel at your strength in dealing with me and at your inexhaustible commitment.

You heard their reports of my diagnosis when I
refused to listen.
Aunt Elaine, you did this all because you loved me unconditionally.
You and the family of fellow foot soldiers ceased
to give up on me, even during my meanest moments. You all stood there, washed and watched my back, held my hands,
paid the bills I created, and
cared for me when I didn't want to believe I
should even care for myself.
You made me appreciate the fact that my life should be lived with dignity and respect.
For that, I pass this light torch onto you. Please
keep it shining.
It has led the way for me.

For: Dianne Giles

Growing from the Milestone

"There's a place for us, somewhere a place for us . . ."

On the dawn of this new
day, we celebrate our
heritage
on the belief that these are our days.
We create history, uncompromising and affirming.
The books written, those in progress, Gay-Straight Alliances as well as the
definitive curriculum meant for teaching and learning,
will document our past,
present and future
contributions.

On the pulse of this new beginning, we
give credence to the Stonewall Riots which gave birth to the gay liberation
movement. We also give credence to the civil rights movement.
It took many injustices
and inequalities to fuel us on.
From this moment, each
death will be remembered.
Their blood poured like oil,
recommitting us to this new
horizon.
We are encouraged and empowered to never forget
sacrifices made by Harvey Milk, Essex Hemphill, Pat Parker, Assotto Saint,
Audre Lorde, PFC Barry Winchell, Matthew Shephard, and legions
upon legions
of political activists born to give our breath its heat.

At this moment, golden with infinite
potential, hating us needs to stop!
Our best defense is being ourselves.
We march on courageously and unwavering.

On this meaning of . . . life, liberty and the pursuit
of happiness....in our shared hearts we are this new beginning.

On this day and beyond, we etch in all minds
that gay, lesbian, bisexual, and transgendered
people are helping to build this world.
We share our contributions with honor.
No one grants you freedom. You just are!
From this moment we stand and state our purpose which we have always
known. From this moment we say we are inspired to take this road with more
determination. Hating us needs to stop!
Our best defense is being ourselves.
We march on courageously and unwavering.

On this day and beyond, we etch in all minds
that gay, lesbian, bisexual and transgendered
people are helping to build this world.

No one grants you freedom. You just are!
From this moment we stand and state our purpose which we have always
known. From this moment we say we are inspired to take this road with more
determination. From this moment we stand proudly.

Posthumous

I wish I could finish my brother Dennis's doctoral dissertation.
All his coursework is completed.
I see his writing tablet has begun to fade.
Our mother thought we were going to finally have a "doctor" in the family.
"He can take care of my ailments" she declared.
His sociology degree would have been added to the numerous citations and awards he garnered in between his three-day-a-week dialysis treatments.
Throughout the past 20 years,
Dennis drove himself back and forth to work, the treatment satellite and school. He lost weight. and gained knowledge.
He studied hard and long. He never once questioned,
"Why me?"
Scholars like him challenge the impossible.
He knew he wasn't the only one who suffered with a kidney failure. Dennis talked loud, fast and with sound judgment.
We listened.
Intelligence was his gift.
In the end, we hoped he would have walked across another stage. Maybe he did, and we are still cheering him on.

No Mystery to Love

I'm living out my fondest
fantasies being with you.
Simply put, I'm in love with you.
There is no hesitation
in affirming that statement.
I am growing more into
you with each waking moment, in ways that tell
me,
there is no denying
that you are the one
for me.
I have never felt a need to stray or cheat on this
love, to find fault with this love,
or to live it out through another person's lens
in order to see you
differently. No one can take
your place!
I will never let that
happen. Does one get a
prize for loving so strongly
and securely?
Yes. At the end of the
day when the night
meets
the falling sun,
I applaud us both for not
running and for saying, "Thank
you God" for another day of
loving.

The Escape

Free condoms greet the patrons as they enter the club. Posters promoting *Safe Sex*, highlighting *No Drugs* and cautioning, *No Needle Sharing* adorned the walls.
The dance floor feels like it is swirling with the pulsating music. Everyone feels no pain.
Jacob knows tonight might be the one when he again explores that sexual part of himself with . . . whomever. This rush only occurs about every two to three days. Suddenly Jacob is dancing so close to this guy, a complete stranger. They are kissing as if they are lovers.
Tongues are glued into each other's mouth.
The music stops and they are still caught up in the moment. Last Call came and went.
They leave the bar not knowing each other's name, but knowing each other has a hard-on that was about to explode. Jacob's car is steaming from their inability to wait until they get to one of their respective houses.
Whenever the libido cries out, everything else comes to a halt. This scenario repeats itself over and over again for Jacob.
He is amazed that 20 years later he is still alive!

Shanelle's Song

Shanelle's swagger was definitive,
strong and pronounced.
She walked with her
head not lost in a cloud.
Shanelle knew since day one that
she was determined to become a woman. She
fought her way through school and was beaten
by punks who wanted a piece of her ass.
Shanelle epitomized the gender identity
debacle. There were those who couldn't
tolerate
her self-determination in a
society defined by classification.
He was now she!
Her beauty could not be mistaken.
Men desired her whenever she entered the club.
Gerard claimed he knew Shanelle's body was going through a
change. Gerard wanted to believe Shannelle was really a woman.
Cocaine can induce such a sensation.
Gerard smoked more and more that night. He
then felt Shanelle's erection.
Gerard's envy caused him to snap.
Shanelle's neck was broken and her dreams died too.
Gerard's trial set him free.
Shanelle's song still has to be sung.

Walk the Talk

Whenever Belynda talked who wouldn't listen.
She had pioneered a trail of living with HIV/AIDS
that others took and translated into their own power of self-love.
Upon news of her diagnosis Belynda didn't run.
She knew she had to turn this challenge into a victory.
Her baffled doctors marveled, even cried at the strength of her
resolve. Belynda held on to her belief,
"My God won't destroy me. He knows I live to serve him."
Belynda founded the AIDS Action Committee's Who Touched Me
Ministry, and enlisted black churches who had closed doors to people like her.
She felt we needed all forces together on the battlefield.
Through her tenacity and determination, the sermons were refocused and
spoke to the love God had for all his children.
"You can save the person just don't close the door." Belynda said. She used
her own sense of survival as a tool to heal others.
Belynda demanded people inspite of their illness, stay active and not sink
because of fears.
She often vowed, "AIDS will not kill me."
Belynda thought the purpose of her life was to share and she lead through
example.
No one should ever be afraid to speak their faith.
Belynda wasn't.
We have been touched by her and are
blessed. Let's continue to walk.

Immediate Family

Olivia, the oldest by six years,
held onto the arm of her sister
Ruth as they came off the
elevator.
"I still don't trust them damn things. So they can go up to
the thousandth floor and higher! Lord knows if God wanted
you up there with him, he would have called you!"
Olivia expressed these sentiments as she straightened her
hat. Ruth smiled and said nothing.
Their brother Matthew had spent the last three days in the
hospital for some tests.
They were destined to end this visit to Matthew
quickly. Olivia also hated hospitals.

It appeared Matthew's balance had given away on him real bad this
time. Olivia speculated that he finally drank too much alcohol.
Olivia felt she was the authority on life, and her age gave her that permission.
She proclaimed, "I know his wife's death caused this problem."
Ruth, still hurt by her own husband's swift cancer death, spoke to her sister
Olivia in a definitive tone.
"Now, Olivia, Matthew's wife been dead some 20 odd
years. And besides, Matthew and Joshua are a couple . . . ."
"A couple of what?" Olivia snapped. "Gay men in love
and locked in some damn closet?"
Ruth finished her own statement.
"Chile, they are a gay black couple who have been together for the past
10 years.
It's people like you Olivia, that felt the closet should remain shut!"
Olivia let go of Ruth's arm and walked briskly up to the nurses'
station.

Template

My sister passes by our mother's room early in the morning,
and sometimes late at night.
She hears Mother crying. It's one of those solitary
moments. My sister detours back, allowing Mom that space.
However, when my sister returns through that narrow
hallway this time, she hears our mother praying:
"Dear God, grant me the strength to fulfill your mission.
Continue to bring peace and joy to my children. And please don't let me
suffer long and hard for them."

Now my sister has her own solitary crying moment.
"Mom is thinking about her ultimate death" sister ponders to herself
as she closes the door to her bedroom.

My calls to my mom twice a week are always with the intent of making
her laugh at something funny.
"Mom, today one of my first grade students shit his
pants. There I was cleaning it up just like you did for us
fifty years ago."
"Was it that long ago?" she laughs.
I was expecting her to say, "I hope you washed your hands afterwards!"
I always end our talk with a song to keep things upbeat:
"This little light of mine, I'm gonna let it shine."
We begin to sing
together! My other song
is,
"He's got the whole world in his hands. He's got the whole wide world
in his hands."
We are straight for the next day.

Balancing the Imbalance
(People Getting Ready)

"People get ready. There's a train a comin.
You don't need no baggage. You just get on board.
All you need is faith to hear the diesels hummin.
Don't need no ticket. You just thank the Lord."
Curtis Mayfield 1965

No one can tell us we weren't preparing for this moment.
We have strived for it every day.
Discerning souls marched ahead and led the
way. There were emissaries like
W.E.B. Du Bois,
Mary McLeod
Bethune, James
Weldon Johnson,
Sojourner Truth,
Audre Lorde,
Bayard Rustin,
Thurgood Marshall,
Malcolm X,
Dr. Martin Luther King Jr.,
Fannie Lou Hammer.
All of them saw the
light. They flashed it
before us,
guided us, and kept us in much anticipation for a different
tomorrow. We continue to pray and believe that our souls will be rescued.
Finally, that day in our lifetime arrives with President
Barack Obama. The country feels the change, and hungers for the
revision.
President Barack Obama is that tomorrow, today.
But even as this time prevails, we experience great
uncertainty nationally and internationally.
President Obama's words, diligence, and actions will have serious

consequences. His goals describe America's best qualities: the exploration of
different ideas, the embracing of alternative points of view, the call
for optimism,
the respect for and celebration of unity in diversity, and the belief
that everyone should have the opportunity to contribute their talents freely
in the service of others.
We praise his belief in the strength of the American people and in
the promise of the American dream.
However, the affirmation of "We the People," the starting point of our
233-year-old
Constitution, has yet to fully resonate.
We will never achieve the full promise of America until all people are
treated equal under the law. Our fellow lesbian, gay, bisexual and transgender
citizens are still without equal status.
Our fellow lesbian, gay, bisexual and
transgender citizens are still without equal
status.

The train much bring change with the guarantee of full rights and protections
for LGBT
people. These Americans also take care of aging parents, nurture their young
children, and care for spouses in sickness
and in health.
The perfect union can only come when everyone's rights have
been fully supported.
We cry, hug, sing new songs in celebration of your arrival.
Please President Obama, listen to our hearts as you listen to
yours. Lead us out of the imbalance and into the linear path.
Your leadership of change will hopefully assist in stemming the violence that
kills too many black men, and energize Congress to pass and sign into law
the Matthew Shepherd Act on Hate Crimes, and inclusive Employment
Non-Discrimination Act, and federal Domestic Partnership Benefits and
Obligations Act.

Please use your position to confront homophobia, and condemn those who stigmatize sexual orientation. It only fuels the devastation spread by HIV/AIDS. Call for repeal of the "Don't Ask Don't Tell." law and any other legislation that hinders us from moving towards full equality for all Americans. That train is coming fast. Let it be complete with a
profound sense of hope and promise.
There is no ticket needed. Let's all get on board with equal status.

No Apologies

Damian and Crystal sat at this big table directly across from each other.
This particular conference room was going to be used for the spontaneous mediation that was to take place between the two of them.
Damian was rather unfazed, even steel-like.
He sat in a questionable state, couldn't care less about him and Crystal resolving anything.
He considered what occurred "a little freak accident."
The mediator begins the sessions laying out the guidelines.
"Each one of you will have five minutes to present your side of the story..."
"Naw, there ain't going to be no five minutes. I said it was an accident." Damian interrupts.
He shifts in his chair as if he intends to leave the room.
"Please. One second, Damian. These are the rules, and you must be quiet until I finish."
The frustrated mediator completes her delivery. Crystal appears eager to start.
The unfolding of this "accident" took on different turns from her viewpoint..
Ultimately, Damian got up and motioned to leave the room with this parting remark, "I ain't apologizing to anybody.
Her head got in the way."
This was Damian's defense for hitting Crystal over the head with his book as he exited their classroom earlier in the morning.
After Damian left the room, Crystal, along with the mediator and the peer mediator's assistant shared out loud:
"Wow, I can't understand why Damian would treat females like that? I know his mother is dead. However, his behavior is totally disrespectful."
This was an insightful statement coming from an eighth

grader. The mediator searched for the right words, careful not to
say what she didn't know.
"Perhaps Damian is still healing from his personal loss. No one ever apologized to him for taking away his mother." she concluded.

Wise Tale

Winston told me to
take my hat off the
table.
"Didn't your mother ever tell you that could bring you
bad luck?" he proclaimed—as if fathers have no
wisdom in such matters. Winston was drinking his
cheap wine excessively and cursing at everyone. His
elderly mother, who often speaks in a sarcastic manner,
was also being cursed at by him. Winston was even
wishing ill will on his sister who as sick and near death.
"I'll kill anyone
who sits their ass on my new car," he said
touting a gun. The way Winston was carrying
on, I would say I was looking at bad luck.

Beginnings

Fog encroached on the mornings, and mist lingered on
my car windows. Traveling to work at low speeds,
I had to cope with potholes, puddles, and
school buses ahead with their "We take
precedent" stops. I arrived unscathed. Then I
walked down the
school corridors. They were laden with the rising
hormones of young adolescents, their libido-driven
language, the
stares and giggles from girls, and the harder-
to- manage demeanors of conformist boys.
Suddenly, I heard an outburst of "faggot" followed by
laughter,
euphemisms of "nigger,"
and the Spanish word "pato."
These are "shout-outs" to each other, I have to believe.
Your skin can't be too thin, I
thought. I professed to be strong.
I mumbled, I give back to this
community every day.
The verbal chants can't be directed at
me. I sighed relief as I finally sat at my
cluttered desk.
The telephone rang.

The Scar

Grandma still felt the pain.
The scars within her hollered out.
It has been years. Yet still those memories filled her days.
Grandma remembered the threats she made to the other
women in her own defense:

"You damn whores. Stay away from my husband!"

She waged a war with two goals in mind. One was
the preservation of her marriage. The other was to fight "Those bitches."
She claimed they took her husband's money and love meant for her.

She contemplated revenge.
She awakened one night with blood on her
hands. Nightmares haunted her after that.

Whenever my grandmother and her seemingly meek husband
started their up-in-your-face screaming and their heavy
breathing. It was heard through doors nearby and far away.
Yet no one ever came to the rescue.
The timid grandson ran faster away from
it. His youth knew no other direction.

Grandma's husband retreated into a passive mood after each one of the
beatings. My grandmother knew he wouldn't touch her too soon.
One swollen eye still allowed her to cook his meal.

Furor
(The Mayhem of Lights, Camera and Running)

It is reaching unprecedented proportions.
Did anyone else ever see it getting this
big?
Out of the scope of normalcy arises this
phenomenon, known to some as par for the course.
This side of sanity it is not.
In fact, it's like turmoil running on craziness.
How does one distinguish between what is fiction and what is
fact? What is the price of what is being done?
Who really benefits from this ferocious dogged attempt to be
the first to frame this moment?
What can these pictures do for
me? How life altering is it?
Does this move me into a lower heart rate,
or a moderate blood pressure?
After all, these are people that shed waste from their bodies the same way
I do.
Making one bigger than life is commercialism at its best; it
sells. But who really gives a rat's ass that Angelina or Brad had
another kid,
or that Lindsay Lohan had another driving-while-
drunk episode.
or that Princess Diana was seriously thinking
of marrying another man of color?
Could all eyes really want to know who is being chased?
Are our lives that shallow and the shallowness so vastly
transparent, that we want to hide deeply from ourselves? Is the
agenda to catch
someone off guard during an unscripted moment in which they argue,
throw a fit, cry
incessantly, or otherwise act "regular?"
Let's face it, this furor is a luxury not exclusively
germane to reporters and photographers on the celebrity

beat. Do we really want to hear their hearts race,
or to hear that their subjects get their hearts broken just like everyone else?
People are sucking up this stuff like ounces of gold being
offered for free.
Maybe I should position myself in front of my house and stage a
sit-in to protest the lack of AIDS funding. Then I could seek out
those
same cameras. How many photographers do you think would show up?

Investment

Towering over, and never losing sight of other like-minded visionaries, you know the wealth that exists within the masses.
They are forces that assist in moving our agenda towards social change and social justice.
There is no silence to your ascension (as the eighth in line). Your work ethic speaks to your karma.
Belief in peace and prayer are vital parts of your self-actualized being.
Your ability to wrap around God's goodness, resonates with acknowledgment of the mantra:
"For whom much is given, much is required."
Your inexhaustible commitment to advancing the cause of freedom, through education, makes a statement.
Not only are the lives of our youth impacted by your call
to deliver; but the lives of people in general are also impacted. We say with praise that your arrival is for us all.
Your staunch memories of people connect your passage. You know too well that you never walk alone.
I personally have vivid recollection of your presence some 30 years ago. Destined to achieve, you never went off course.
You were centered, chiseling out the monument of self. Northeastern University and Boston College have shared in this construction. From them, you were awarded Bachelor of Arts, Masters, and Doctorate Degrees in Education.
A testament to the excellence you gained through setting goals definitively. You are paving the way as a strong role model who your children Keith Jr., Kayla, and Jordan can emulate and be proud of.
Your climbing hasn't ceased.
You are taking University of Massachusetts-Boston to a higher stage creating a worldwide sense of recognition.
There is much to be said about justice coming to those who walk, talk and hold firm to the principles of righteousness.
Your time spent dealing with breaking down barriers and embracing the truth is paying off.
The planting of foundations started with you. Now collectively, we all stand tall.

For: Dr. J. Keith Motley

Curtain Call

"Focus on your own lines," instructs Ms. Diamond. The theater students are testing a medium about concentration.
Like the hypnotic smell of a sweet perfume, drama calls the soul. Although this is a new aspect in their lives, they go the
distance.
To act upon the writings of a playwright, is like being the pen in their hands.

Ms. Diamond's theater arts students are told to take to the stage and explore their feelings.
"Speak with a sense of authority. Let the breathing come natural."
Orchestrating students to express a visceral feeling can be a task.
"Have you ever been hurt by someone? Let that emotion show at this point,"Ms. Diamond says with blunt force.

Andrew, the protagonist in this play, speaks up.
"Could we rehearse that one scene where I'm supposed to be painfully crying when confronted by my parents?"
Ms. Diamond smiles and answers, "Certainly! But let us see you give it more physical movement with those tears."
What teacher wouldn't take pride in inquiries meant
to make one grow?

Months later the set designs are all in place.
Cast members are rumbling briskly and backstage is buzzing with youthful excitement.
The final project begins.

Each student takes a bow.
The audience is on its feet applauding. No one can question this mass approval.
"Bravo! Bravo!"

The cast members signal for Ms. Diamond to come
onto the stage.
Enthusiastic parents and staff offer extended cheers!
The cast links hands with the director and producer, people whom they know
encouraged their creativity. They move to the front of
the stage.
The curtain comes
down. The applause
continues.

Consequences

Carmen hides from herself.
She can't remember the last time
she did a self-examination.
There are no mirrors hung anywhere in Carmen's house.
Her mother never said, "You are beautiful."
Her own pain and sense of neglect linger.
Minds closed to abuse, prevent corrective forces from
entering. Carmen's father says the only thing Carmen is
good enough for is what her mother refuses to do—suck his
penis every night. Carmen walks to the end of the school
corridor
and pulls the fire alarm.
She escapes into the ladies bathroom with her father's gun.
Because of all the commotion made in evacuating the
building, no one hears the gunshot.

Dodging Bullets

Jorge dashes to the boys' restroom.
The urgency to piss is there; and the
need to cry in private.
Screaming would draw attention.
Jorge was wrestling with the perpetual and
often ugly scars that come from a family in
crisis. Jorge loves his father.
Jorge's dad tells him, "Respect
people as you would want to be
respected." However, Jorge has big-time
issues with his mother.
Her hostile disposition
intensifies when she drinks.
There is no waiting for a weekend or a
celebration for her to drink a six-pack of Budweiser.
She play fights with Jorge, and hurts him.
He senses she is dissatisfied with her own life.
Jorge can't understand why his parents argue so much.
They don't even live together!
Jorge's 13-year-old mind wonders about his own life.
Will he be like his parents—in love at first, and then angry at the end?
Can he survive a war-torn community where bullets
have young boys of color as their target and
where no ice-cream trucks can come down his street?
Should he run away;
or take some of his dad's painkillers and numb out his own pain?
Jorge's girlfriend is no help.
Even when they make out in his
bedroom, he is distracted.
In his mind, Jorge hears his father hollering
over the phone at his mother.
Jorge figures maybe taking the medicine will alter his thoughts and
everyone will fade out.
Jorge wipes his eyes and exits the bathroom.

Invest

We celebrate with Eileen and Susan.
Your spirits are consistent and truthful.
Your commitment to social
justice
and total equality for all is real.
We break bread together
often. As we feed
ourselves, souls are also
enriched. We honor the work
you do—
like preserving the earth
and nurturing young minds.
You share your well read books;
and your progressive
initiatives
which bring people together
for the good of sisterhood
and brotherhood.
Networking and securing stronger alliances for the "cause"
is how you spell your name.
We stand taller today; because you both take us to newer
heights through your friendship.

If We Were Girlfriends
A Message to My Brothers

If we were girlfriends, we probably would have been the first ones
out on the dance floor at Simone and Greg's wedding.
The men would be drinking the free booze excessively and talking about
who won the latest football game. They would be wishing it was on
TV at that moment!
—Why does saying 'I do" have to run into the hours of other people
who are having fun
and wasting enormous cash?" the guys would ponder between sips.

If we were girlfriends, we would have screamed in frenzy
whenever we saw each other, like even from across the street. It would have
been a natural expression that flowed from us.
Believing and saying "I miss you" has no attachment to anything
other than the truth.
If we were girlfriends and a man was to hurt one of us, his death would be
executed by simply not dealing with him anymore. This sisterhood revenge
thing would be so mandated.

If we were girlfriends, our friendship would have been linked
back to kindergarten,
similar teachers, and the flirtatious-like girl
who tried to steal our first loves.
We would have known about each other's first pimples and
we would have seen each other naked more than once.

We would have obsessed about what made each boy dump
us, Was it the next pretty face that entered the room
or the girl who gave it all on the first date?
If we were girlfriends, I would have worn your
dress. You would have worn mine.
We would have shared stockings, lipstick, make-up and even
cried over the same guy.
"Gi-r-r-l, how did I let that fine Ronald get out of my reach?"

If we were girlfriends, we would have praised one another about the good choices each had made
and seldom mention the bad.
If we were girlfriends, we would have talked about our first
"period" or our delayed one.

The late icon of black gay literature, Joseph Beam, called me his
"girlfriend";
because he felt our friendship would last a lifetime.
Beam felt men bonded over sports, competition, and the
ability to leave someone with no regrets.

If we were girlfriends, nothing would be better than shopping all day. This would have been topped off by eating from each other's plate, cursing the diets, and then calling each other later that night
to plan the next day's activities.
If we were girlfriends, the need and desire to be in each other's
lives
would have been a no
brainer. How else does one
grow?

Solidarity

The wind
changes, but not
our hearts.
In fact, they both beat with a sense of
contentment. Our courageous spirits never falter.
Our commitment to friendships is concrete.

Our challenge to transcend paths others will not
take, intensifies self-discoveries; and we benefit.

We are strengthened by our unconditional
love, the force that continuously reinforces
this union.

Malignancy

The shots were heard around the
world. Screams punctuated the quasi-
silence. No one listened.
In Louisville, Los Angeles,
New York City, even in Providence,
distrust is rooted in the questionable
verdicts given to those who kill black folks.
Amadou Diallo was murdered by four white cops.
Four policemen, 40 shots! That's 10 bullets per policeman!
No one shouted, "Stop, he isn't shooting back. He doesn't
even have a gun!"
What happened to aiming for the lower
body? Amadou carried a wallet, which told
no lie.
Four policeman, 40 shots. 10 bullets per policeman.
Their unique power came with a sense of
responsibility. To be protected by their force is an
obligation.
Strange, they walked free.
Amadou Diallo was buried with no
apologies. The city remains still, for now.
The disease of distrust continues to fester.

Memory in Motion

I remain numb.
I conclude it's a functional phase.
I still breathe, smile and cry often;
or, in some cases, very openly at the mention of his
name. Roy's mother Jean has a new picture of him in
her kitchen. Jean and I sit there in this room each
Thursday afternoon.
We smell the aromas left behind from numerous dinners that fed our
beings. It has been 17 years since Roy transitioned home.
Yet deep in my heart I feel him and all others who joined
him—Like Belynda, Bill and Thomas.
There was also Steven
who I was adamant about the correct spelling of
his name
and about his not-too-secret love for me.
But what about those three deaths that occurred in one year?
They were my grandmother, my brother, and my godson
whose murder forever haunts me.
I have to believe the embodiment of their souls lives within me.
Maybe it's the weight of their laughter,
their spirit lighting up my house,
or the energy from each one of
them pushing me to my
tomorrows.
I guess, in my numbness,
I still breathe, smile and cry often.
That's life.

Pantheon

Frantz Fanon once said, "Make of me always a man who questions."

Critical thinking aside,
am I missing a point here? Black men not
acknowledging each other is tantamount to not hearing
themselves.
Vincent and Michael saw each other in the gym's locker
room. Yet, neither uttered a word, nodded, or even farted to
show they were in the same space.
Life couldn't be that cruel to you.
We have been rendered invisible by
others; but how can we remain so with
each other? We shy away from intimacy.
If you haven't been shown how to
love, you can't express it.
Are we black men and boys so afraid of our proximity to
death, that we
don't want to establish any bonds?
Does dodging bullets help our defense mechanism?
As black men and boys we believe no one can love us but
our mother.
She sacrificed to have us.
We still wear mom's rag around our
head, a woman's stocking no less.
Those doo-rags and wave caps do what to protect
us? Are we intent on our own self-destruction?
America is doing a superb job at it abroad.
Who pays for our "safety?"
How safe are we when the odds are stacked against
us? As black men and boys we seldom
achieve our necessary and rightful passage
into social, political and sexual maturity.
Sometimes the pervasive question surfaces,
"Are black boys forfeiting their lives to remain boys?"

Look at the inordinate amount of
black boys flunking out of school
and playing games when they come back. Dads walked away.
Some black dads failed, ran, and kept on
running. Whose footprints can we follow?
Stereotypes are images we feed into.
Prison walls are swelling with our sweat.
There are too many courtrooms with us on trial and too many
memorial tributes speaking about short-lived gunned-down
lives. Guilt, shame and denial are imprisoning our souls.
Petty street crimes are contributing to our spiraling demise.
Predictions suggest we can't do anything else.
It's almost like we are bordering on the nadir of
depression. No one says it;
but society's ambiguity towards us speaks to
their attitude, which is conflicted at best.
In celebrations they attempt to reach out to us with one hand; but they
often keep the other hand in a clenched first, as if ready to strike.
Check out the star basketball and football players.
Black boys see the duality and it intensifies their demons.

We black men, as our legacies to black boys,
must fight against conditions of oppression
and not allow color or poverty to impose one's fate.
We must rise up, take back our lives, and know
that our legacies are created by us.
Should present day history be written by someone
else? We know our truths
to be buried in lies.
No one looks for soldiers who have never fought their own
wars. What worthy temples can we say we have built?

When I Stopped Kissing My Father

When I stopped kissing my
father roofs and ceilings fell
hard upon my shoulders.
In the middle of the
floor,
no one experienced the pain but me;
self-pity calls out for such recognition. Distance came between us
as I carried my message which
now defined love to his new
embrace.
Mommy couldn't wait for her kiss and hug combination;
one without the other an incomplete welcome.
Daddy smiled as mom and I exchanged so much
energy. It freed him up.
Compensations step into spots never
filled. No one knows how age and years
begin to separate one from foundations built to shore
one up.
When I stopped kissing my
father, his love faded.
When I stopped kissing my
father upon his request,
I couldn't ask for anything else.
When I stopped kissing my father,
love had a newer meaning called
restriction. When I stopped . . .

Perform

"You are my friend, I never knew it then."

In your plays, each scene pulled us closer to examining
ourselves. You left no mysteries unsolved.
The characters portrayed their lives with certainty and conviction. They
were much like you and the people at Mattie's Grille, which gave us a slice
of black life in a Smokey Joe Café.
You wrote the scripts to numerous plays for us to view.
We couldn't turn away from the unsettled souls searching for a
means to an end. Everyone has a mission--- to find one's purpose.
Thomas, your powerful play "Brother Red" drove home the fact that the AIDS
virus was a family matter.
You believed that if we tackled this one together, the other wars
wouldn't be as harsh.
Malcolm X lived through your incarnation of him in "The Meeting."
Some people said it was as if Malcolm X gave you his blessings to recreate
him on stage for so many years.

You and I would analyze life with all its complexities;
and we often wondered if the world could get any worse?
We felt it could either be the bullet, greed, or plain
old ignorance that would make us victims.
We called upon all those who died before us;
we knew our very existence meant standing on their
shoulders. They increased our vision and made our journeys possible.
We even cursed out those individuals that mercilessly
didn't bother to challenge the world.
"Why else does one exist?" We would say.
We wrote from some of our deepest pains. Everyone listened.
Who couldn't relate?
We cried and laughed at our mistakes. We vowed that our lives would not
be the same without each other.

Talk about going through the fires.

We actually put them out only to have them start up again.
We knew what to do for each other. As Essex Hemphill has
said so poignantly, "When my brother fell, I picked up his
weapons and never once questioned whether I could carry the
weight and grief of the responsibility he shouldered."

Thomas, your generous
heart created so much joy.
Your death is not in vain;
your voice will be heard
through our voices.

You were passing the torch along.
Whether we could aim or be as precise as you, will never be the question.
We all know you have fallen and the passing
ceremonies marking your death
did not stop this war.
So we, who are the Writers of Color Workshop, New African
Company, Poets of the Horizon, Sisters and Brothers du Jour,
the Grimes
Theater Company, your numerous friends who felt so
fortunate to be called that, and your loving family will all take
to the stage and continue to resonate with your passion.

Who Saves Us?

Thomas never told me how sick he was. Maybe he felt I couldn't save him.
Thomas and I promised to tell each other about the bad as well as the good
times. We were soulmates who shared everything we could.
I thought he and I had spoken of each other as being the sustaining force in
each other's lives.
We also had our writing, shared thoughts of making love, and shared our
composure while drinking wine.
He knew what made us happy; but he must have
forgotten. Maybe he felt his sickness would pose a
problem.
"You already have Belynda to think about," he once told me.
I felt the push;
but I went to see him
anyway. What really saves
us?
God must want everyone to be up
and out of bed whenever He calls someone
home. Why else do we get those calls about
death
so early in the morning or so late at
night? No one can sleep after such news.
Or is it fear that rocks the bed?
My partner said, "You were such a real friend to Thomas."
I literally cried myself to
sleep. I am still crying.
I know each death chisels away at my life.
We are meant to feel weakened by the call of
death and cry for ourselves as well.
Lack of strength leaves us feeling at a loss
—like a part of ourselves has been
removed.
The emptiness vacillates between highs and
lows. How does one begin to heal?
What eventually saves us?

We can't depend upon others to hear our cries of sadness
or to remember their promise to console us.
I waited for two such calls. Did they misplace my phone number?
We can't assume everyone expresses loss in the same
way. Some would rather not think about it.
Worry is the absence of control.

Great Minds

Once people know about me and sense a perceived calm,
they ask if I know whether or not Nikki Giovanni herself as well as
Aretha Franklin's talented musician son are both gay.
I must admit, I haven't written the "Who Who's in Gay
America." People think that we gay writers know each other;
simply because we explore and write at length about one's sense of
freedom and love.
I met Nikki 35 years ago.
I was still searching for a definition of myself.
I didn't say gay as openly as I do today.
Also, my knowledge of musicians spoke to their need to play in
an idiom that they believed the souls craved to hear.
I heard that they spend endless nights jamming and
emptying their hearts out in haunted cafes and clubs. They made
these venues ripe afterwards for a night or two of comfort with
anyone, anywhere.
Fast forward to a different time when singers hid behind a mask.
Gay activists of the 1990's were adamant about iconic singer Luther Vandross
"coming out."
They felt his words professing love between a man and a
woman were smokescreens for his real passion: men loving men.
So they pushed him to say he was gay with a simple "Yes."
He barked ferociously.
Ah! They knew then that it was fear, and not this love he
sang about, that prevented him from entering the club officially.
It was too late when his death silenced that incredible voice. Luther never
became an official member.
It's really not a recruitment process as much as it is a like minded pursuit.
People know that there is strength in numbers.
The late Joseph Bean was a very insightful and sensory person. This gay black writer so
eloquently wrote, "Black men loving black men is a revolutionary act!"
How great is that?

Surrender

Triggered by the sudden early morning invasion, Miguel and
Juan couldn't fall back to sleep.
Forces new to them had stepped into their world.
Depending upon which one of these identical twins
you asked, change was about to happen.
Their minds were registering some
disruption that was going to cause a move.
No one else could speak for them; so Miguel did

"We are good boys. We don't do drugs. We go to school."
He pleaded for mercy as the
police ransacked his home.
Their mother Evelyn and 18-year-old sister Kamalish stood watching in dread.
Tears flowed from everyone's eyes.
Miguel shielded Juan.
Then he repeated, "We are good boys. We don't do drugs. We go
to school."
His train of repetitions startled the policemen.
Miguel and Juan couldn't express the fact that they have autism. The police
sensed something was different about these two very frightened 14-year-olds.
Miguel eagerly said, "I know where she hid it." Perhaps he did this to save
himself and Juan.
Bags upon bags of marijuana were found and hauled away. Suspected of drug
trafficking, the twins' mother and pregnant sister are handcuffed and taken
away.
Miguel and Juan are placed in an ambulance. From that moment their lives
began to crumble. Each day the boys struggle to stay afloat.
Now they wake up in a motherless home.
Their now present dad has to share his new life, his girlfriend, her ten-year-old
daughter, and a much smaller living space.
No one wants to let Miguel and Juan's interdependent lives fall deeper.
They already had to give up a sense of normalcy. Will their security be
restored?

The Weight

Liam wasn't trying to save his soul anymore.
He didn't even want to talk to the new school counselor.
"Who the hell does he think he is?"
Liam could be heard saying as the principal attempted to silence him.
"I don't care. I ain't talking to nobody, black man or white man!"
Liam was determined to drown in his sorrow. He has been doing this for the past six years.
Liam's grandmother, the sole breadwinner of this family, struggles with connecting the dots--- the missing links in both grandchildren's lives.

Liam's younger sister, Kathy, was also about to give up at
times. Her voice, the inner one, told her not to.
Kathy at least goes to the after school program on a regular
basis, communicates with her aunt in Springfield, and spends a
night or two at a local friend's house.
Her diversity of activities alters the shift from depression.
Liam isn't as fortunate.
He physically and verbally assaults other students. He
throws makeshift objects from where he sits in the room.
He denies each incident.
Witnesses compel him to surrender to his own
madness. The urgency of his behavior produces the
same results. Grandmother comes into school. He is
given a suspension Two to three days later he returns.
Same demeanor—wimpy, bullying, clinging to his last bit of hope.
"I didn't do it . . . this school is so gay."
Finally, the counselor sits him down.
After an inordinate amount of dead silence,
Liam slowly utters, "I create a lot of stress for my family," tears
appear at the
corner of each eye.
"How so?" the counselor queries.
Silence.
More tears and a heated voice, "My mother wouldn't have died if I

hadn't run away."
Liam is finally sharing a glimpse of details surrounding the long-reported suicide of his mother.
Liam was taking responsibility for something he thought he caused. The counselor sighs and begins the session that could hopefully
shift the weight.

The Habit

My mother utters, "I have so many people writing to me begging for money."
She had experienced another week with an overflow of letters personally addressed to her.
My mother complains, "I can't understand it; why do people keep writing to me?"
I retort, "Mom, all that stuff is junk mail."
"Yeah, then why are they personally typed with my name on them?" She queries.
"Mom, they got your name from one of your credit card companies."
"Chile, you know I ain't got no credit card anything. These people just keep on writing me.
I even have one here from the President." I'm too afraid to ask which president?
The lion in her won't let it go. Ah! Could it be that old age thing again?
She often believes the person next door is listening in on her conversations and informing outside folk that she has retirement money stored in her bra.
"Mom, excuse me for saying this; but you need to deep-six the shit!"
Never a saint to a little curse word or two herself, she proudly states, "Shit nothing! I even received something addressed to your brother Dennis today!"
I almost fell from my chair laughing, still balancing the phone. "Dennis? This is proof. He has been dead nine years," I say.
A sense of shame comes over me because of my outburst. My laughter turns to a tear as I hang up!
Mother continues to open her mail.

The Past Returns

Leroy figured he was a pro at saying goodbyes.
He just wouldn't say a word.
One time, he got up and left before sunrise,
drove himself out of the maze that an alcohol-induced night
can produce, and landed in his own bed.
He believed it was his own bed.

The old 1960's hit "Never Can Say Goodbye" was a particular song which fit
Leroy's lifestyle.
Leroy, Roy to some, never talked during his rituals—the
rites of passage so to speak.
He let his body communicate with the instant nameless conquest of the
moment. Whenever the affair was over, it was a done deal.
No repeaters. Time had a way of presenting
newcomers. Fifteen years later he waits for an answer
He has no patience
His nerves speak to
him. Tears flow.
He counts the days.

Power

"Whenever I dare to be powerful—to
use my strength in the service of my vision—
it then becomes less and less important whether I am afraid."
Audre Lorde 2/18/34-11/17/92

It rained the night of Audre Lorde's memorial service
at English High School.
I wanted to believe that God was crying with us.
No surprise that there wasn't a seat available. Mostly women in
attendance.
They sat shoulder to shoulder.
Some rested their bodies on the wet steps inside the auditorium.
Monique led us in a rendition of "His eyes are on the sparrow
and I know he watches over me."
Audre's own words prefaced the evening event:
"I am a feminist woman, lesbian,
grandmother, and warrior
in love with a white woman.
There is no question about my existence.
I create no boundaries to hinder my movement
forward. I fought the causes
that attempted to stop me;
and I can't be."

Resonance

"Good to have you in these times." Joan Armatrading

You sing those masterpieces,
high and low, but never deafening.
Because in the music there is also a
message driven home by the contagious beat.

In our talks are those clear
thoughts, like meaningful lyrics.
In your hold of me,
the harmony surrounds us and cements the
moments.
You have listened to your heart and can't deny
those feelings; you speak, sing and give praise!
I was crippled by not responding.
But your songs have freed me
up. So I confess: I love you too.

The Love Affair

I left you years ago to make
other discoveries.
You missed me, I believe.
My wings had a need to spread and
face other challenges.
I didn't think much about you.
It was about me.
I knew others would continue to show you
love. Yet, I have never forgotten you.
When I return, we meet.
There is such fondness
and remembrance.
I hear many voices praising your strength and your
beauty. People come from miles away
to stay with you,
and you welcome them.
I walk with pride knowing they too share the love.
Some people's lives were started with you.
There are generations of families who speak of
you. They recognize you for giving them
opportunities way beyond belief.
They will never leave you.
You, with your arms open, are their Ellis Island
home. You have it all.
I come home more frequently to you, New York.
You are one of my true loves.
This affair has to be rekindled.

Tribute

"Them that got shall get. Them that not shall lose . . . ."

I speak about your life, your death, the mountains you
climbed, the paths you paved, and the roads we traveled.
You wrote the truth according to our history, from
Stonewall to the present.
You spoke out about life's complexities. You were in touch with your emotions
of pain, despair and the numbing outrages that helped you become you.
You fought your drug addiction and came out a stronger gay black man.
The self-imprisonment ended.

You personified pure honesty. It shielded me from the lies,
the deception.
In the end I wanted to protect and sleep with
you. There was such a need on my part to
experience
your cries at night, and cradle you until the next
day. I kissed your Kaposis Sarcoma lesions.
I listened to your fleeting thoughts of hospice versus home
care. Your family and I would have taken your place
numerous
times.

Four female friends of mine sent me cards. Condolences were
not meant to be silenced. I told everyone about your life and
death while I was busy cashing checks or lifting weights.
Even my grandmother said she had circled an article on AIDS, so she
could share it with my nephew, her great-grand.
This wise old lady had lived long enough to know pain and to understand my
suffering about your loss and others notwithstanding.

I typed your obituary on your personal computer. Your spirit
worked through me; there were details we couldn't omit.
God gave me time to hold on to
you. We made love to each other's
words.
Your family praised the way you lived, their support
was insurmountable.
Your farewell had to be in sync.
Your mother and I have adopted each
other. We live to never forget.

The Final Bell

The excitement registered with rapid murmurs amongst
the audience.
Apparently, these eighth-grade students were feeling
restless. On this day the teacher, acting as the guidance
counselor, instructed the students to select five high
schools.
"Beware, you might not get into your first or second choices."
How could one not be nervous?
"Suppose your first choice is the only one you want?"
a frustrated Emmanuel uttered out loud.
The teacher answered, "Please keep in mind, the School
Department would rather you and your parents decide on the right
school for you. Giving yourself choices shows you have done some
research."
Could this be the last hurrah?
Many of the students in attendance can't see beyond the next
minute!
Asking them to envision themselves in a high
school eight months from now is, at best,
daunting.
Their fears are real and many.
Their sense of denial is rampant and interruptive.
However, they are encouraged, prodded, and otherwise
outright forced to bend a little in order to do a major task.
That is
what we do.
This bell will ring no longer.

We Still Leave A Legacy

Each death chisels away at my life; no other impact has
entered as strongly.
Now, no cries can go unheard.
There is a newer purpose to these days. The aftermath
tends to linger longer this time, allowing lives to be
reassessed. We have become more in touch with our own
mortality. Revelations are meaningful timetables to this
discovery.
Those who die in silence often experience more pain.
To bury one's dreams is to let go of life. Our larger mission
is to complete tasks that have been left incomplete.
Our greatest weapon against fear will be the collective
intelligence and love willed to us through our higher power.
When the deepest of emotions has been put in check, we will
have acquired the sense of touching and caring for ourselves,
sources
of true deliverance.
The enforced censorship of our private affairs will never censor
my love, our love, the movement.
There are beams of hope and faith directing us, keeping
our search infinite.
This is one battle we'll win.
We have been handed the torch. Our march is for
us. It is for them. It is forever.

No God—No Boundaries

Pearl Bailey once said, "People see God everyday. They just don't recognize him."

From Harlem to Dorchester, the "N" word is spoken as if history never occurred.
You hear it in the music of the day and on the silver screen. Lives were destroyed by a system of evils emanating from its conception. It is a system operating outside of God's law, a system with no moral boundaries.
We ran for cover whenever this word was imposed on us by others.
We knew it meant death in one form or another. We vowed to study war no more.
The battlefield is still mounting. No one corrects them.
Girls and boys, especially the African-American youth, give hipness and credence to the "N" word.
I take a deep breath every time I hear it. Whites and others are confused.
If they were to use the word, they would be called racists.
"We don't mean the same thing," Dwayne, now growing an afro hair-do, proclaims.
"These my dawgs, my boys. It's our right to the passage or something like that."
Those in authority, those with teachable skills, say nothing to cease its usage.
Down long corridors and under watchful eyes you can hear the word.
It flows like water.
It is a constant reminder that these youth don't recognize God within themselves or in each other. No God—No boundaries.
Teachers say we have important responsibilities to contend with, such as teaching and learning.
Those who fought long and hard would say character building and development of positive self-esteem are just as important as the teaching and learning of

academic subjects.
They cannot be traded off when the going gets tough for
teachers. Moral consciousness is frozen.
Massive challenges should be embarked
upon to remind the young that
we cried and died
when called the "N" word.
Let us try and fight
to make sure that we never hear it again.

The Aftermath

During the process, silence was registering;
or was it fear?
Sylvia became speechless.
The doctor was moving her lips, and, Sylvia heard--- nothing beyond
"You have the first stage of . . . ."
How could she not have seen the signs?
Then Sylvia thought, why confuse the situation more? It is here. Live with it!
Her emotions were beginning to rise. Some were singularly devastating
and others were calmly acknowledging.
"Ah! Maybe, I can take that world cruise, come back and file bankruptcy;
Or, perhaps, I can order up all those magazines I often read in the grocery
store lines without paying the bill." Sylvia ponders to herself.
They were silly thoughts.
It came time to reckon with the truth. It could be a death sentence!
Sylvia proceeded to read her bible, a daily staple in her
life. She sipped some more coffee.
Without hesitation, she
called her beauty salon to make a hair
appointment. No point being unpresentable for
her new book signing at Walden Books.

The Visit

It has been long and overdue.
Memories were so vague about how the last sojourn was; it felt like starting over again.
In preparation for Mother's official "re-visit," the refrigerator was stocked with presumed favorites.
The evening's meal of barbecued chicken was baked with just enough seasoning. Potato salad was prepared that day of arrival to let every ingredient settle. A tossed salad contained home made dressing. Asparagus was sprinkled with fine, preserved feta cheese.
The guest room was hotel clean with new linen on the bed and Neiman Marcus mints on each pillowcase. Bath towel and facecloth were coordinated to match the freshly painted blue and white walls.
Drapes flowed from the ceiling to the floor, the way the magazine showcased them.
A lavender air-freshener permeated through each room. The whole house sparkled. The cleaning lady had come the day before and left with her seal of approval. Tentative plans were ironed out a third time: first night would be dinner with
Barbara, along with her delicious chocolate cake and precious dog Amber, in tow; the
next morning, Mother would rise to Joe's famous pancakes, coupled with home-style scrambled eggs and sausages (both beef and chicken); and of course, orange juice would fill the new glasses.

When Mother entered the house, she took one swift look around, grimaced a little and uttered, "Is the heat on....?" Sister and brother smiled at each other. The thermostat was moved up higher, a second time.
The visit began.

Paradoxical

Back when the GI bill rewarded every completed stint
with a guaranteed house and an education, it was better than flipping burgers.
My father served in the Army twice
and we still lived in the housing projects.
Mommy's black eyes
spoke of the "combat" Daddy fought at home
in between stints.

"Don't ask. Don't tell."
"Which truth should I keep to myself?" PFC. Barry Winchell probably asked.
He was entrusted to die for his country; Barry met his enemy at home.
His questionable gayness never said he couldn't shoot a gun or defend our
country in global conflicts.
His generation inherited wars.
Now, who tells his history of a mere 21 year-old?
"Don't ask. Don't tell."
Barry told, and
death was his reward.

"Don't ask. Don't tell."

When President Clinton told how he
betrayed the highest office, he kept his job.
He'll have his self-serving
life, his royalties and the
legacy
of "boosting the economy."
"Don't ask. Don't tell."
Clinton's exit song said this policy is "whacked."
Is justice delayed, justice
denied? No one is telling!
Barry told,
and death was his reward.

The Spirit of Remembrance

To say goodbye to Kofi was difficult. When did we ever say hello?
My nephew and I hadn't spoken
for any great length of time.
Suddenly, his troubled and disconnected 29 years ended. Our last visit with him only lasted two hours.
That particular dialogue was laced with Kofi's anger.
It occurred during the long arduous ride to his father's interment. Kofi refused to see beyond his own feeling of abandonment.

Kofi and I were not only separated by three states;
but also by a family dynamic that spoke to a shattered history.
Anticipated and yet not seen, was the misplaced attempt by Kofi's
generation to take us to the next level.
Kofi can't take the entire blame.
His parents' crossed signals created for him a self-imposed
strategy for survival.
At times my nephew's cries for help went unanswered.
Masked by his father's own constant fear of death, Kofi's illness
went undetected or denied.

My mother whispered to me at her grandson's memorial,
"Should I say they both died owing me money?"
I said, "No, God will take away one or two of your pains in exchange." We smiled and held each other's hands tighter.

It's hard to bring closure to life.
He was connected to us as a son, friend, nephew, brother, cousin and grandson.
A part of him will always remain in our hearts.
To close Kofi out again,
would not be in keeping with the spirit of remembrance.

Landscape

No denying the beauty of the clear pond
—inviting but
not too deep, having
the illusion of an endless wonder.
There's enough space to walk around
it. Briskly.
Run in
tandem or
alone.
Trees towering over are as ancient as this land
itself. The shade they create renders sighs.
Almost out of nowhere you came riding your bike.
My eyes captured your upper shirtless-muscle-bound torso with those blue
spandex shorts fitted like glue to your thighs.
Did I notice a
helmet? Hell No!
I will come to this pond every
day for the sights.
How could one miss the blueness!

My partner Joseph Jackson and I.
Keeping the Legacy Alive!

www.ingramcontent.com/pod-product-compliance
Lightning Source LLC
Chambersburg PA
CBHW050653160426
43194CB00010B/1918